AGAINST COMMUNISM

A TRACT AGAINST AN ABSURD IDEOLOGY

I0407862

Tarl Warwick
2017

COPYRIGHT AND DISCLAIMER

TABLE OF CONTENTS

INTRODUCTION

I: Communism an Evil Philosophy

II: Marx Wrong about Primitive Communism

III: Communists make Dumb Excuses

IV: Abuse of Workers and Corporatism vs Capitalism

V: Witnessing Communism's Failures

VI: Direct Democracy and Communism's Faults

VII: Central Planning does not Work

VIII: Anarchists and Socialists Arguably even Worse

IX: Communism never Helped Anyone

X: Gated Communist Communism

XI: Conclusion

INTRODUCTION

For those who have actually studied the impact of communism on the world, it is as sensible to relegate it to the realm of lunacy as the concept of trying to go to the moon in a swimsuit, but while the path of communal non-ownership has largely passed away and now comprises a pitiful minority in the world, it is always helpful to remind ourselves in various forms why the ideology should be shunned. If we have a field littered with glass shards we frequently tell one another to beware of them, but if we clean most of them up, so that they are a rarity, it still makes sense to be wary and ask others to consider the same, lest they slice their feet. Communism is like this; a rarity, but one still capable of dangerous acts, especially as newer generations rise which have never lived under its auspices. Indeed, the areas of the world today which have a more positive view of communism are invariably those places which never had communism; Western Europe, for example; the self proclaimed elitists there can't understand why their Eastern European brothers, who suffered under this system, would oppose it, because they do not have personal experience with the USSR, which is akin to other regions outside of the land the Soviets, Maoists, or any other group held for any significant time.

Today we look around and there aren't any communist regimes in operation (which does not surprise me.) Cuba is now under a form of admittedly bad but livable socialism (and is beginning to just barely westernize) while China uses a mixed authoritarian society which only has a remnant of and the name of communism to its ownership. North Korea has devolved even further than Maoism ever could and has become a strange almost monarchic land in which a hereditary line of juche masters have created the most strong of centralized systems.

AGAINST COMMUNISM

Anyone expressing pro-communist tendencies is very likely to be beaten half to death if they're doing it in a part of the world where the suffering of communist systems is still fresh in the mind of older generations. Meanwhile, in areas where communism never smeared its blood-tainted rhetoric and began its inevitable campaign to suppress all productive classes and enslave them to misery, people often around my age pretend that Che Guevara was anything but a dirty, bitter bigot and had redeeming qualities- sure he did, if you count the fact that he gratefully got killed before he could massacre more civilians, I suppose that counts as a redeeming quality. Or we might consider Stalin, who was so egocentric that he ended up alienating the Maoists, driving China to craft its own political and military sphere, and subsequently attempted to kill Tito, only to be on the wrong end of the gun, so to speak- for Tito probably poisoned and killed Stalin in retaliation for such imposture.

Thus I will speak at some length on the subject of communism; why it should not be forgiven for its past, and why I am extremely glad that it seems peak acceptance of far left ideologies in general and communism and socialism in specific has already begun to wane as the next generation rises to where mine was a decade ago. The result I think of this will be extremely good for the world; as the older Millennials and younger Generation X see their children growing into young adulthood, the same newer generations appear to have utterly rejected political correctness, cultural Marxism, and the things I am most embarrassed about as a Millennial myself, and have adopted a sort of generally populist ethos forsaking some of the worse qualities of the old guard, moralist right wing at the same time. I believe Generation Z will be as great as the last great generation for the world and will accomplish much. Optimism at last!

I: That Communism is an Evil Philosophy

Here I give little more than my own moral opinion and will give it an equally subjective moral basis. I can delve more into policy and historical fact (or at times what is generally inferred as fact) in subsequent sections. It is important that the reader know where I stand philosophically.

The three most butcherous systems of human endeavor which have been spawned from the hellish pits of the darker minds of our species were all marketed as and, perhaps, originally meant to be, benevolent; I speak here of organized religious zealotry, state fascism, and communism. Of the three, it is communism that sets itself far, far apart from the other two as the most noxious and murderous; the death toll communism resulted in over the course of a few short decades dwarfs the death toll of fascist movements by nearly an order of magnitude, and religious zealotry required a thousand years to kill the same number, although in the much longer span of time perhaps its own murders are numerically superior.

When we observe a system to judge it we must separate principle from action; it is not enough to judge for example a religions' dogma, we must also judge the actions of its adherents both in totality and in whatever age we happen to occupy in time. A religious force that spent centuries as a pacifistic movement of extremely peaceful monks may suddenly be usurped by an era of re-interpretation that leads it on the path of warmongering and conversion by sword; the early Christian movement was largely separatist and partially pacifistic towards outside groups until it became the state religion of Rome and was corrupted by its imperialism and statism. Communism, at its core, is not an evil so much as a delusional and utopian philosophy that is incapable of existing in its pure form- its pure form is far too unstable and deviates far from mans' biological reality of competition and ownership, which is innate and drives evolution. This should not be seen as negative in its normal level of existence, only when it is manipulated to support things like an arms race and other nonsense that could wipe us off the planet entirely (which communism is as guilty of as any western system!)

When I observe the things said by self proclaimed communists today I see a large number of mistakes made in their claims. They claim that pogroms and famines never even happened under communism, that the Holomodor and the murders of the reign of Pol Pot never actually occurred, and that most of what we non-communists believe about those periods is carefully crafted western propaganda. At the same time, I hear often that they disown Stalin, Pol Pot, and others, on the basis that they were not following "real communism." So which is it? Should we exonerate them because they committed no crime against humanity, or should we merely remark they were evil but not communists at all?

Then while they excoriate the suffering of the Juche ideology in North Korea, they claim that Kim Jong Un and his predecessors are merely pragmatically resisting western imperialism. They go on to complain about imperialism in all forms while exonerating the post-imperialist boundaries of the USSR which after all were build by the actions of the Russian Empire in its period of greatest conquest. It is all very confusing to hear them talk.

Che Guevara, also both proclaimed "not a real communist" and yet applauded for butchering some civilians and trying to orchestrate the overthrow of several states, is perhaps the most amusing, since the same people proclaiming themselves to be citizens of the world, who love everyone and merely want to "liberate" them from "evil" "capitalism" ignore the fact that Guevara was a notorious bigot who occasionally enjoyed the private ownership of luxury goods from the western world.

Depending on whether we only count purges, pogroms, and assassinations, or whether we include death totals from communist movements and policies they implemented in a wanton and unintelligent manner, the ideology at large has killed at least several tens of millions of people, and possibly above one hundred million people, in less than a century of time. Mao was the worst when famine is included; his war on song birds starved much of China- but Stalin, that old bogeyman with his constant declarations of being the sole representative of "real" communism, probably slaughtered more people directly, and would have gladly killed more of them if the western world had not amalgamated into a military alliance he knew he could not underwhelm through force alone.

Of all the proclaimed communists of the last century though Pol Pot may be the most outright evil of them; this bastardized miscreant killed most of the skilled or trained individuals in his nation of Cambodia because he was convinced that a quasi-primitivist system of communal misery should supplant industry altogether, piling the skulls of famine and purges so high that it reshaped some local landscapes there. His tyranny was so supreme that the Vietnamese, also run at the time by communism, got tired of dealing with him. In a remarkable turn of events, the United States government actually recognized (due to the political climate) Pol Pot as the legitimate leader of his people- probably one of the darkest blots on our own history, truth be told.

There is a common claim that communists make that should be addressed here; to me, it seems almost like they admit defeat when they use it. The claim they sometimes make, of course, is that "real" communism has never even been implemented in a real world system.

I disagree. I say that communism will degrade into a Stalinist, Maoist, or other offshoot sub-system due to instability even if you achieve a stateless system through some technological or social means. Let me, though, entertain the claim, and pretend that I agree with the concept and that "real" communism has never been implemented (and that no serious attempt has been made to implement "real" or "genuine" stateless communalism.) Then we have another stain on the credibility of their ideology; the philosophy itself is so weak, or so unnatural, or so stupid, that even communists themselves cannot get it to work. Like a convoluted Rube Goldberg machine, it breaks down at the slightest perturbation in a world where chaos is frequent and disasters over the short span are likely and over the long term are inevitable.

I say that organization is innate and thus stateless systems will not work, and that likewise competition is innate (in the evolutionary sense as well as cultural) and as such, a system in which competition is lacking is inefficient and, where it is altogether absent, little to no progress can ever truly be made.

Communism suffers from being thus at once both delusional and continuously subject to the use of tyrants who preserve only its name, because it is impossible to formulate a stable communal society. It is against human nature in the biological sense. I do expect that communist revisionists will eventually attack the theory of evolution and the cultural anthropology attenuating it to declare that competition is not innate, by using some form of newspeak to muddy the waters.

II: That Marx was Wholly Wrong on one Central Principle of Note

Karl Marx was very much like the so-called scientists of various zealous religious movements today; instead of attempting to observe and document, he launched off on a crusade to amalgamate and interpret anything that he could from mans' past to reinforce his general theory of primitive communism. That is, he presumed that his premise was evident and then attempted to stretch observation beyond all bounds to support it. This led to the general notion Marx developed (agreed to by Engels and others) that the original hunter-gatherer societies of the early stage of mans' development were basically proto-communists with a form of communal ownership.

Marx did not live to see this theoretical statement utterly torn apart. There is a reason that no sane academic course teaches Marx or Engels alongside more modern scientific thought; indeed Marx was the product of his era, and held the same general beliefs of his contemporaries- generally speaking the intellectuals (if you can even call Marx that) of the 19th century gazed upon the world, felt that it must have been better in the past, lionized the past- especially far antiquity- as a sort of golden time from which man had degenerated, and spawned a thousand theories as to why that had happened and how it could be reversed. Communism, thus, in the sense of Marx, is better compared to any other period movement or school of thought alongside those who felt early man was imbued with psychic powers or those who recognized the cultures from before Greece or Rome as savages but noble ones, and lauded them in their pastoral nature.

Early mankind was not communist. That much is clear

even when just regarding the physical remains of some of these groups. Neanderthal burials had not yet been explored in the time of Marx and nobody realized that, it seems, they buried objects with the dead that appear to have been owned (or at least primarily used) by the dead. That comes even before the more organized hunter-gatherer societies of post-archaic homo sapiens. Marx could well have studied more cultures than he apparently read about and understood the same thing, the same problem which stood in the way of his hypothesis making sense; we can even observe (from slightly afar!) tribes today which have never been substantially contacted by the outside world, in which we can see, with our own eyes, the rudiments of private ownership at least of small objects like weapons or clothing, such as the Sentinelese; a very small tribe inhabiting a few small island regions off the coast of India. They remain in the stone age even today, with nothing more advanced than fish nets and wooden spears, and apparently each own their own weapons.

Private spaces in primitive architecture literally appear in some of the oldest known semi-settled cities. Catalhoyuk was founded in 7500BC- three thousand years before the Sumerians built a shack and almost 5,000 years before the Egyptians built their first mud brick pyramid. These people couldn't have been rudimentary communalists; the city itself was quasi-communal but each family (nuclear or extended, it isn't entirely clear) had its own more or less separate living space, and clearly its own ancestral shrine (where the remains of the dead were placed) along with its own cooking and sleeping area. Almost ten thousand years ago, well on the way back to utter savagery, mankind already had what is more likely the rudiments of a concept of private or at least family ownership. It is far more sensible to state that mankind has ever increased his level of organization along such lines, from the self to the familial to tribal to the proto-state, always with a sense of self and, as we may term it, selfish ownership. It is natural to man.

III: That Communists make Dumb Excuses

I spoke already of the claims of communists that "real" communism hasn't been attempted (or implemented- they claim both from time to time) so that particular excuse does not need to be restated. I already spoke at length of the biological problems with communism in "Improving the State" (another manuscript I wrote on social and political topics) so that, too, needs not be echoed again; it's a side argument of sorts.

There are other problems with their arguments though. It would take a long time to name them all so I'll fixate on just two of their other significant and patently wrong claims here. The first is social, the second is fiscal.

The social claim is that communism is some sort of apex; a "stage beyond" capitalism, or the current state of the world, or of some nations. This shares the same problem that so many other ideologies have had through time, especially those developed around the same time as Marx existed. The concept of social evolution in the sense that Marx apparently held it, along with others (Marxism is not solely to blame in this sense, and wasn't the first system to make such a mistake) is straightly wrong. The same mistake I speak of here is shared with biological evolution; people have come to the belief that it revolves around advancement when really it revolves only around change- there is no advancement per se save for one very specific and purely human advent, namely intellect as it applies to technological capability- humans can artificially advance with far greater fervor (once their mentality is developed enough) than genetics can; we are more like a virus in the social sense than a mammal, due to our extremely quick social and cultural ability to change, and due to our tendency to screw ourselves in the process.

AGAINST COMMUNISM

In the social sense, though, the mistake is strictly this; that each system fundamentally considers itself the apex, to the exclusion of all others, which it generally ranks into hierarchies. It is innate for man to do this. I developed my own hierarchy of political systems based on their long term stability- that this is at least two parts opinion to one part observation of historical reality means that there is certainly room to debate the point. I simply say something "can work" and "has worked" and leave it at that, without claiming the system to be perfect; another, as yet untested system may function better.

The second claim as I said is fiscal; that communism is just or that it can operate in the economic sense. I say that communism is basically a two part being; the stateless and "pure" communism its adherents desire and the statist, centralized communism they seem to generally get. In neither case, does it operate fiscally. Centrality becomes inefficient, bloats up, and withers- we see this even in supposedly free market regimes (which are generally corporatist) as well as in communistic movements. As for stateless communism, it would be a godsend to any enemies of the culture using it, since they would quickly find it impossible to fight a war. And in either case, compulsion will of necessity rule the day- even in a stateless system the communists will at least exile those who wish to forsake it, forcing them off of what then becomes communal lands.

Indeed, here it is a statement of communism at large; and an important one. Namely *neither the pure communism that communists desire and say they want, nor the communism they decry as fake, will ever work, because it will destabilize whether or not a state exists to administer it.* Time and time again communism has at least been attempted; depending on which communist you speak with at any given time, they will proclaim that either none of these now-extinct systems were actually communist, or that they were and outside interference (those bourgeois imperialists!) destroyed their capability to function.

Let me then combine this claim with one of the aforementioned problems, namely the social one. If communism is an apex predator, the ultimate form of humanity, and something both stable and noble, why did it spend a century being destroyed by movements which were supposedly inferior in the ideological sense? If communism was morally superior and apparently more efficient, as communists have tried to claim to me, why did both free market and corporatist regimes alike manage to denigrate it so badly in the economic sense, as well as the social sense, and why did western propaganda win the day?

The answer is simple; the Marxist has made a grave error in their reasoning; communism was suggested at a time long before western, free market (really semi-free) systems implemented proper policies on monopolies and worker protection. Marx didn't think of these things and merely encouraged the working class to rise up and either jail or kill the upper classes (and often the middle class as we saw in Russia) or to exile them or disabuse them of all ownership. To Marx, the justified response of a peasant tired of working their fingers to the bone was to beat his plow into a sword, metaphorically and literally at the same time; but then we observe the plight of both humans and the economy under communism when it was attempted and the result did not help the working class nearly as well as even the more corrupt corporatist regimes of the western, civilized world. One can't blame the communists of that era like we can those of today who have evidence their beliefs are wrong; it was little more than a medieval style peasant revolt with firearms and manifestos added in, and a small intellectual core leading them to their early graves in the form of people like Lenin.

IV: That the Abuse of Workers they use to Justify their Movement is not caused by Capitalism Anyways

To be sure I am not excusing the west of abuse- I claim personally that abuse abounds and should be stopped; but the communists' idea of how to end it is based on the false premise that the bogeyman of capitalism is responsible for what too much centrality actually caused- indeed, the same centralization we observe in proclaimed communist regimes! What worker abuse can exist in a true capitalistic system, in which government oversight is specifically relegated to cracking any monopolies or trusts that arise to continuously promote competition? None can; communism is not needed to protect the worker when the market is, by and large and continuously, always a place where businesses compete for workers and for sales, forcing them to lower prices and raise wages. Our primordial problem (continuing even to this day due to the governments' own intervening in our economy at large) is the reversal of this staple of capitalism, in which instead the worker competes for the business and large firms compete only with far smaller, weaker upstarts rather than with one another specifically. We have cases where seemingly competing restaurants are owned by the same larger firm- thus there is no true competition. A loss in one franchise is outweighed, generally, by a subsequent rise in the other franchise, both benefiting the same corporate firm. A dishonest tactic to be sure.

Corporatism is not quite as bad as communism; there is at least the dim hope of lifting oneself up a socioeconomic class or two- in extant communism such classes are strictly defended by the political and military elite (and in pure communism there is equal misery for all!) I've done this myself- I was born into the lower class, otherwise known as "living in a slum apartment built in the 1830s with working class parents in a tourist town." I've managed to build up my own income to roughly middle class levels- which makes me extremely fortunate. I accomplished this not by relying on the government but through the use, mainly, of the internet and realizing there were several largely untapped niche markets for certain types of literature. Would this have been possible under communism?

The answer is "maybe but probably not." Specifically, in a pure communist system I'd be trading books for bundles of carrots or sheet metal for my one room hovel. Under centralized, extant communism (the type that inevitably actually exists) I'd probably have a decent brutalist apartment for a while until the red guard comes and throws me into prison for having unauthorized political and spiritual opinions. At some point they might release me, or maybe they'd put me in the rock quarry and work me to death.

Corporatism of course is not as good by far as capitalism. Our current system though is hampered by (and all the population too) not too much capital, but by too many bureaus, regulations, and high tax and spending policies- indeed, such that it resembles Stalinism-lite or something of that nature. It has little to do with the system we employed for the first hundred years of our history as a nation. We began as an exceptionally decentralized, virtually zero-tax nation which became a corporatist system in the late 1800s because of trusts and monopolies. Rather than simply implement a constitutional reform to ban such behavior so that competition would repair the situation, Theodore Roosevelt (who I admire) made the well intentioned mistake of formulating a progressive era which eventually made the problem worse. I think he cared, and meant well, and short term much progress was made- but long term it harmed more than it helped, and did little to stop monopolies and trusts, which continue to this very day in new forms. Enormous and almost always international corporate bodies simply split into smaller, virtually non-competitive firms to increase their own holdings off the paper so to speak. This is more like the fracturing and proliferation of ministries and bureaus and semi-autonomous mixed model firms under latent Soviet economics than it is the model employed by the United States prior to the gilded age.

Our workers here suffer because the government causes problems whenever it attempts to solve them. It also has hero syndrome and sometimes starts problems on purpose to look moral when it pretends to solve them. And each additional strangulating layer of bureaucracy or intervention makes it harder for small businesses, upstarts, and entrepreneurs and easier for multinational corporations, because the tax code is convoluted- the tax rate paid by businesses here is actually extremely high, it only becomes a piteously small sum when accountants and lawyers are used to exploit loopholes that it contains- something easily done by large firms and nigh on impossible for small firms let alone people building drones in their basement or computers in their garage.

Thus our systems' difficulties; low wages, stagnant growth, high prices, and the necessity of constant imports and trade deficits are the fault not of free market capitalism but its absence. Communists seeking to unite workers to help them would be better off becoming constitutionalists or libertarians and realizing that the centrality of our system is ultimately the cause of their problems, not some mythical bogeyman of capitalism, and that their crude depictions of fat plutocrats only exist because of corporatism, federal supremacy, and central governance, not because of a free market.

V: That We Now Have over a Century of Communism to Observe and can Witness How it has Never Operated as Communists Desire

The closest thing to a functioning pure communist system that we have ever witnessed is perhaps amusingly the deeply religious Amish or something of that nature. At no time in world history has a truly communal system arisen for more than a short period and then only locally or regionally, before it militarizes, or is usurped, or devolves into abusive and totalitarian ways.

When the communists compare their utopian, pure system to those that actually sprang up over the last century, we can perhaps reason why communism ever failed to be implemented- the human drive towards competition is both a major factor in our evolutionary success as well as a major factor in our difficulty creating truly stable cultural and political systems; it drives us to advance and succeed, but then drives those in a position to do so to abuse the same systems that have been made in order to benefit personally, usually to the detriment of others. In a total vacuum, utopian systems are all well and good; pure communism, borderless anarchism, benevolent dictatorship, and so forth- but in no case do these systems remain in place, they are inevitably denigrated in some way and usually to a large extent.

Utopian ideas are a pipe dream in our current world. When we thus see libertarianism, we see an ideology that I myself admire, but have to criticize frequently because so many of its proponents do not understand the concept of infiltration and have no problem with limitless and mostly uncontrolled immigration. This force would destabilize even a successful attempt at implementing a purely libertarian state and within less than a generation it would be far different.

Communism became the worst and most butcherous of philosophical systems because the corrupting tendency of competition (which is in normal circumstances not corrupting at all) operates upon it not once but twice. First, it strives not to be eliminated when communism is implemented (which reduces its efficiency and causes the kind of black markets and graft we witnessed in the Soviet Union, for example.) Secondly, it causes those individuals in the transitional period towards this utopian system to seize control personally through force or subversion of some type. This natural tendency is constrained under more stable forms of social and economic systems, but not under communism.

The communist thus looks back and can only remark that Stalin, Mao, Pol Pot, Guevara, and others were not "real" communists. But that is beside the point and doesn't matter; if we take them to represent communism, it is a philosophical path that slaughtered nation after nation to a degree so horrifying that most formerly communist states embraced only the most virulent pro-western sentiments. If we observe them and say they were not real communism, we have instead a simplistic observation that communism *can't be implemented* at all because of the fundamental evolutionary nature of our survival. Communism is, strangely enough despite the claims of its proponents, the most warped of the philosophies to arise from an era in which man wished to return to a golden age that never existed and created experimental social systems, seeking to solve problems by introducing even more complexity into society where complexity was often the cause of the problems they themselves wished to solve.

But we can compare the plight of communism (pure or

impure, again, it matters virtually not at all) to other systems and we can perhaps see what creates stability or destroys it.

Monarchism in its pure form, as a blood-lineage dictatorship, certainly has existed and operated properly. However, monarchism tends to be short lived- there is no guarantee in the pure sense that the next ruler is not insane or a warmonger. In a less pure form, a system in which the monarch is limited by a church or legislative body or council of oligarchs, there is no guarantee that either the monarch or the second limiting body is sane or effective. That being said, even this generally outdated system is superior in stability to communism.

The most stable states are those with constitutional systems and representative governments, or so it seems, almost regardless of the state of their fiscal systems; when problems arise, it sometimes is the result of espionage or of the grand chessboard between the US and Russia (and now sometimes China or the European Union) at play, where sock puppet regimes are made or broken at a whim in a style not entirely unlike that of the constant deposing and crowning of lords and kings in the 15th century.

Even a semi-representative and corporatist system outperforms impure communism with its central planning. And even an extraordinarily constrained libertarian or anarcho-capitalist state, in time of crisis, will outcompete and out-organize a pure communist system. When we witness this we witness the reason why communists never actually managed to implement what they themselves declare to be the best and final human philosophy. In that one specific claim it almost becomes a bit like a religious cult as well.

VI: That Like Direct Democracy, only Small and usually Homogeneous Communities can even Approach Communism

When we see working direct democracy in the world today it generally takes two forms; the first is in small and largely homogeneous states like Switzerland, where a highly literate and armed population makes many of its decisions in a democratic nature and relegates the state itself almost to secondary importance within a constitutional framework. The second is localized democracy- we might think of town meetings and local actions taken in communities around the United States or in some microstates. Direct democracy, though, doesn't work in larger nations at the national level very well, because the interests of different groups of people are often so radically different. If the USA, for example, were a direct democracy, it is likely that the rural minority would be perpetually put upon by the urban majority and it wouldn't be long before there wouldn't be any agriculture in our nation any longer that wasn't controlled by some subsidized corporate monopoly.

Communism is quite similar. Taken locally it has seen at least some limited success- the anarchists and communists of Spain before being crushed by Franco did manage to hold territory, defend it, and govern their local actions without being obliterated for some time- but these pockets were beset by outside forces and never gained enough traction to take command of Spain at large. And if they had, Spain would have fallen quickly from a marginally developed nation into deep third world status, because the same system that is capable of operating locally cannot be extrapolated nationally unless the nation is a microstate and everything is local to begin with.

AGAINST COMMUNISM

This may be the greatest weakness of many otherwise potentially working systems of government, none a better example than communism and its anarcho-communist and similar offshoots. A revolutionary group takes hold locally, and things seem to work; the community is likely more homogeneous economically and ethnically than whatever nation as a whole they happen to reside in. Over time they expand, and their expansion eventually weakens and destroys these weak systems and their ability to properly regulate the state, or rather the population if the concept of the state has been largely or completely abolished.

To govern large territories, order must be maintained- communism in its impure form can do this but only through intimidation and constant militarism as we saw under Stalin or Mao. Pure communism lacks the capability to do so, and will eventually lead to a patchwork of schismatic movements; so-called libertarian communism, anarchocapitalism, syndicalism, primitivism, and so forth- these systems can't govern large areas with heterogeneous populations and economic needs, because the pseudo-democratic action employed to "govern" is never capable of working for some collective higher good.

In the end, the only systems which are able to create large areas of control are either tyrannical to some degree, or representative systems (a sort of collective itself in some ways) with a constitutional background in lieu of democratic order. We might even think of communism as a type of warped, corrupted direct democracy- it shares some of its tendencies including, as stated, its inability to reach out beyond the local or at best regional and maintain any real stability in its operations. A communist microstate based on a single way of life- agrarian, industrial, tourist haven- is capable of working, but as soon as it expands outwards and includes all of the above, the industrial unionists and farmers will fight over subsidies or land or access to resources, or the working class will fight with the tourist-catering merchantile class, or something of that nature. No significant attempt to maintain them all for the benefit of the state can be taken because under pure communism there is no state at all. And under the ways of Stalin, Mao, and similar professed communists, constant attempts at central planning almost always destabilize the economy at large anyways, making this local and regional infighting secondary in importance.

I referred to the Amish prior. Here we have a semi-collective culture which operates in largely autonomous conditions here in the United States, but its actions have two differences with pure communism in its general form; it is a religious (theocratic, almost) community, and while land is semi-collective it is split up on a tribal level between families, which do not share land or (usually) home but rather much of the productive material drawn there from. Their system is actually more wide-reaching than any working communal structure to ever exist, possibly because of their shared ethnic lineage, language, and religious beliefs, and partly because of their oligarchic style of council system, in which a handful of religious elders more or less dictate moral strictures to the population- which is rarely schismatic, although it did lead to a few less morally constrained offshoots over the last century.

Because communism emphasizes the homogenization of populations it can never truly adopt the aspects of cultural movements like the Amish that actually allow stability to be maintained beyond the local level. It would be difficult indeed for communist movements to adopt aspects of theocracy or representative or constitutional systems, and even harder for a communist population to be armed since counter-revolutionaries would constantly hamper the collective.

VII: That Central Planning does Not Work

Central planning is not solely limited to communist forms of government and society- indeed, most so-called free markets are at least partially planned at the central level; this centrality can take the form of a nation's government directly building something, or granting money to a private entity for similar projects, or it can be done on a state, provincial, or local level. Under most communist regimes central planning was singular- under Stalin virtually anything was carefully crafted by the Soviet government and its bureaus through increasingly strangulated processes until efficiency became a running joke. Over time some private business was tolerated but it was still heavily intervened in.

China, today, is probably the best example of the disconnect between more efficient for-profit private action and the actions of investment that occur when jobs are not lost nor a profit lost by the handlers of money when there is a centrally planned grant or loan system in place. China has invested in both forms in infrastructure and urban development to an enormous degree; and so long as China continued to exhibit swift economic growth, any empty and unused infrastructure was quickly filled in. Now, dozens of rather large towns and cities sit mostly empty, buildings and roads built for no purpose degrade and cannot be maintained, because central planning has severely overestimated the continued viability of their mixed model economic growth. This is roughly the left wing counterpart to private speculation that occurred here in the United States prior to the great depression, and has essentially the entire world sitting on pins and needles worried that an export juggernaut will fall away into a downward spiral as it begins to run out of fuel, so to speak. Their concerns are valid.

AGAINST COMMUNISM

The problem of central planning is that the bureaucrats and government figures responsible for dispensing funds have every motive to greenlight large projects and present them as both viable and profitable while simultaneously they are given no motive to avoid wasteful spending. The former stems from simple human tendencies- namely graft and corruption- we can observe its sapping effect on even the best economies, and in communist or mixed systems it is more prevalent, or so it seems; the United States sadly is slowly becoming a mixed economy too, so I wouldn't be surprised to see our lot worsen before it improves unless we implement drastic overhaul. The latter stems from the tendency of party insiders in China to inevitably avoid any condemnation and never to lose their permanent bureau jobs unless they dare speak out against higher ranking party officials. The party, of course, calls itself the communist party of China, even though China hasn't technically existed under communism since the 1980s and is one of the few states to actually move towards a better economic system after having devolved into abject leftism.

Here in the United States we refer to centrally planned projects as slush funds or bridges to nowhere; our nation is rife with such nonsense- some senator or representative manages to insert some stupidity into a spending omnibus to grant their own constituents a library that won't be used, a road that nobody will drive on, a bridge that leads to a largely uninhabited island, or a statue nobody asked for, all to ingratiate themselves on the population, secure re-election, and make it look like they've done a good job for their voting base. The government grants untold hundreds of millions of dollars every year to academia too, often that money gets frittered away on useless "studies" that have less to do with academics and more to do with crafting low-cost "academic" practices to justify the grant while squirreling far greater monetary sums away to build stadiums or to offer students their choice of useless elective courses by hiring overpaid celebrity "professors" who teach them about women's studies or the history of bread crumb art.

Europe is also increasingly centrally planned. Most legalism in the European Union no longer even comes from the already strangulated national governments of its member states but rather from the seat of power there in Belgium- specifically Brussels, the capitol of what I hope will be a quickly degrading and doomed project that hasn't helped the Europeans or anyone else other than bureaucrats and other human scum sitting there pretending to represent the common good. Central planning apparently extends beyond the purely economic and is indeed just the fiscal counterpart to actual fascism- a system decried openly by most of those actively practicing it. When leftists cry about fascism, they are too blind (or dishonest) to see or admit that these economic and social systems they themselves vote for are a form of the same far more than the traditionalists, libertarians, or outright nationalists that they worry so much about.

There has never been a time in human history where central planning has worked- even medieval and renaissance lords typically encouraged the free movement of merchants between their territories, with relatively little abuse, so they could obtain luxury goods at lower cost, and to help promulgate alliances. Today, most so-called free trade deals ever struck are just another layer of government intervention replete with legalism that doesn't even pertain to trade in goods.

VIII: That Anarchists and Socialists and so-called Social Democrats are Just as Bad if not Arguably Worse from Time to Time

Communism will always be an insane and failed ideology, but what can we say of its proponents today? Since the Chinese are communist in name only (the Vietnamese too), and because Cuba is centrally planned but wavering and now absorbing massive sums in tourist money due to the end of the US embargo there, and because North Korea is simply a state that has existed in a constant war footing for half a century while being shut out from almost all global trade, where are these actual communists? I will speak of Starbucks Marxists- the smartphone-wielding self proclaimed proletariat warriors later, but perhaps actual communism, pure communists, should be discussed.

This relatively small movement appears to be almost entirely relegated to states where the population never suffered under communism- as I stated for Western vs Eastern Europeans, because they never directly existed under the suffering of a self proclaimed communist regime (Stalinism) they have less of an aversion to it- instead, all abuse that they ever perceived came from governments which stated that they bitterly hated and opposed communism- naturally, a few young and delusional individuals caught up in the "us and them" false dichotomy of reigning western politics thus project communism as an image of fairness and equality as compared to what they perceive of as the evil, imperialist, abusive west with its corporate firms. Try and tell them that corporatism is closer to communism than it is to free market capitalism and they will rarely understand your (very true) point and continue to ramble, often strangely about Ronald Reagan, Margaret Thatcher, or perhaps "that old sellout

AGAINST COMMUNISM

Gorbachev." I very much enjoy the 1980s and its figures and goings-on, but most of their fellow young people are clueless.

But far left ideologies are inevitably bad for everyone- this extends well beyond merely communism either pure or impure- it extends to communism with a smiley face (democratic socialism) and communism-lite (socialism, another term for corporatism.) Indeed, if anarchists and communists in their more pure form realized what socialism entailed they'd oppose it with great vigor, instead they seem to regard it, often, as a stepping stone or a "move in the right direction" towards what they imagine will be the eventual dissolution of the state altogether into a sort of technocratic postmodern collective.

This will never happen; communism can't stabilize long enough to abolish the state and actual communists who have ever held power know that it's just another political identification to use as a cover for syndicate-style crime and graft, like any other system. Something closer to true communal existence would be more easily achieved through free market capitalism with trust busting and anti-monopoly laws and a severely constrained constitutional system- indeed, a few brighter minds eventually leave communism behind as the failure it is and embrace some sort of anarchocapitalism, which is a step removed from sanity, as opposed to the leagues-removed communism with its centrality.

Democratic socialism is quite literally the personification of "think of the children"- that ever present disguise under which the most dishonest dregs of society clamor for more power so they can control others and access their money. This same retarded excuse is dragged out to justify even the most ridiculous laws or ordinances, the most insane proposals are given an almost spiritual facade in such systems, in which sweeping statements are made about some higher collective good or morality or thinking of the less fortunate- the less fortunate never actually get lifted out of poverty or sickness under such systems though, because the absence of the poor and helpless would render democratic socialism unnecessary and vestigial.

Anarchism is even more strange; here we have groups of people opposing the existence of a state (with or without collectivism) but who mass together in mobs and act very much like a sort of quasi-organized and self proclaimed state military force, attempting to make others miserable. I speak here of self proclaimed anarchists, who consider even the slightest rudiment of police action or private business to be a form of fascism- idiotic movements like antifa with their hypocrisy and near constant state of violence.

Actual anarchists are arguably even more hopelessly lost because they apparently do not understand human biology or the concept of evolution. Much like the far left academics have become a post-science movement and now declare sex chromosomes not to be indicative of sex, I expect anarchism to eventually begin disregarding evolutionary science altogether because there is no way to re-interpret it as supporting their attempt to degrade human organization to below efficient levels. Anarchism gets it right when it acknowledges the abuse of states ancient and modern, but apparently disregards the concept of constraining them in favor of doing away with them so that a new state can form automatically in its place, usually under mob rule or in the fashion of a military takeover (which is what any pure anarchist society will quickly and inevitably experience.)

IX: That Communism Never Helped Anyone

The communist, looking back at a century of self proclaimed communist regimes inevitably falling apart socially and economically, has to deny a lot of what communists once embraced. Communists embraced Stalin, now they have to decry him as a horrible warmonger whose sadism was totally separate from his economic ideology. Communists loved Che Guevara until liberal movements shifted public opinion against bigotry- because Che Guevara was more bigoted than almost any traditionalist is today. Communists adulated Marx and elevated him to a station substituting for godhood, but now debate over which things he got wrong.

This is the confused state of communism today- and because of its lack of capability, it has caused nothing but suffering. All traditions and philosophies are malleable; communism has simply morphed over time- from an on-paper theory based on misunderstanding human history that stressed quasi-anarchism as an end result, to an industrial style of governance indistinguishable from corporatism (indeed, industrial communism in the vein of Stalin was a reaction to first the second world war and then the atomic standoff between east and west), to other forms today. Regardless of which of these variants we regard, they have all failed completely.

The failure is more complete than that of a collapsed economic system or organizational difficulty- these facets of human systems are occasionally present even in the best of systems; from time to time there will be a drought or a plague of locusts, or an epidemic, or society will have to address some major question that causes (sometimes for decades at a time) social stress. Communism has failed on a more central basis as well in addition to these normal problems.

AGAINST COMMUNISM

That is, that communism has actually managed to fail on the most basic level of development- literally nobody has ever been helped by this ideology unless they were within a governing body or happened to be a fairly high ranking individual within a communist military or police force. Communist nations never supplied their lower class with enough food beyond starvation level, and then only with great difficulty in efficiency and with massive graft and corruption. Its business system encompassing skilled workers, academics, and so forth, was muzzled and similarly treated, with scarcely more access to the fruits of production than the poorest. It isn't until these communist systems abandoned communism in everything but name that life began to improve- Vietnam abandoned its communist ways and is now a fairly powerful state in its region. Cuba recently began to largely abandon communism (in both of these nations the label remains!) and now is growing more quickly, slowly reversing decades of poverty. China uses a mixed economy albeit one governed by authoritatianism and censorship of a massive sort. Russia is in some ways now arguably more capitalistic and socially libertarian than the United States, and is far more so than any state in Western Europe save for Switzerland or Iceland.

Communism has been abandoned because it causes misery and holds back human progress- there is an additional facet though; systems must be malleable, and the more strangulated by bureaucracy a system becomes the more difficult it is to keep up with society at large, which then uncouples from it ideologically and screws up the entire game. We've seen this before- we now run these same risks in the west because of corporatism and carpet bagging and government overreach that has begun to resemble some of the more mild authoritarian policies of the USSR.

AGAINST COMMUNISM

Communism is like all other utopian ideologies in that it neither operates nor fulfills its promises to the same groups of people it inevitably must target to take hold in a state. Communism in the USSR was prefaced on the intelligentsia strangulating the government and encouraging the lower classes to take up arms against their better-off neighbors. Communism in China was prefaced on one militaristic group forcing the others to the side on behalf of the proletariat. The situation is similar in all other cases; Pol Pot was a radical agrarian man and shunned even the existence of industry. Cambodia remains economically backwards because of his actions.

In none of these cases did any of the lower class peasants participating in their "liberation struggle" see a significant expansion in their quality of life. In the great depression, many Americans were suffering and lacked proper nutrition, fuel, and then-modern technology and access to it. The same was true over in Russia. After half a century, most Americans enjoyed proper nutrition, access to all manner of technology, and increased wealth all around for all but the least fortunate- meanwhile in Russia, the poor were still quite poor, only now they had a few sub-standard electronic goods and a decrepit Soviet apartment that took months or years to obtain through all the paperwork of an inefficient centralized system.

Today communists are overjoyed to point to the slums of Detroit and laugh about capitalism's failure- but the failure of the rust belt doesn't exactly coincide with their claims. Indeed, it was the movement of manufacturing to more efficient locations and subsequent skyrocketing unemployment that screwed those regions. In the much larger rust belt of former communist states, the same occurred on an order of magnitude above that found anywhere in the west. As always, government intervention creating booms and busts, not a private fluctuation, was responsible here- over there, it was central planning.

X: Gated Community Communism

Now we come to the communists of western gated communities. These trust fund holding whiners are among the least intellectually developed individuals one can behold- but they remain convinced that they possess almost superhuman intellectual capacities and will gladly tell this to you. While typing away happily on their smartphones about the ills of capitalism, they gladly suck down the most sugary capitalistic beverages and, while rambling about the mistreatment of workers in the west, they inevitably do so while wearing clothing that is the product of poorly paid agrarian cultures supplying cloth fibers to be assembled by child slaves in Thailand, India, or China, which is then re-imported to the western world as part of a world trade scheme.

On an intellectual level I can respect someone with a quick wit and who likes debate- that includes even many leftists, and a few outright socialists I have encountered- but the number of modern day communists who are capable of holding a discussion without devolving into baby talk or violence is astonishingly low. Often, they don't seem geared to want debate anyways and merely ignore you if you challenge their echo chambers. I do not mean to say that many virulent political groups tend to ignore those who criticize them- most do- but it seems prevalent among communists self-determined to a far larger degree than with any other group I have encountered.

I've known communists before; a few in the real world, mostly on the internet; I tend to assume any random anonymous individual professing this system is as likely as not just trying to yank the chain of right wingers and won't consider anything they say to be necessarily indicative of the prevailing opinions of actual communists, but there are some which I have spoken to and can determine are both real individuals (actually who they profess to be) and actually believe in communism as an ideology, in several variants.

In all cases these individuals exist in nations which have never existed under communism. In all cases they were not impoverished. Several were wealthy, many were from the upper middle class. A few were from the working class and appear to have adopted these beliefs out of anger at not being wealthier.

I think this is probably important to mention; I have a sneaking suspicion that a great many declared communists are either just angry at those who have succeeded (they often seem to direct their anger more at the productive and wealthy/wealthier than at the super rich which inherited wealth or merely get fat and plutocratic manipulating money- the renting and banking class that is), or have internalized anger at themselves for their apparent inability to succeed. The US government is partially to blame for setting the stage for communism and socialism, by letting the economy decline and spending the prior decades rambling about how we existed in a free market that hasn't actually existed since the early 1900s. When these young communists observe their misery, then, they can only blame it on the system that those responsible for their lot (or so they believe) have adulated and professed to support.

For the communists of wealthier backgrounds, they continue in their wealth and assert, often, that it is acceptable to be wealthier so long as one strives towards the eventual abolition of such economic rungs. It would be a rare upper classer who strives to abolish their upper class existence and most of them seem to take up the name "communist" either as a dating strategy (to be 'interesting' or 'unique') while professing vague dogmas they don't fully understand, or in some cases, as a form of rebellion of sorts (although I can't for the life of me understand how an ideology born out of the mid 19th century is a symbol of youthful rebellion- it hasn't been since the period of the US Civil War!)

Gated Community Communism (GCC as an acronym) is the result of sheltered and often marginally wealthy suburban kids growing up in a sterile suburban freak-land often with helicopter parents seeking to rebel, when the only thing they have left to rebel against is essentially the system our politicians have pretended to support for a century without actually supporting it- namely, free market capitalism. If these GCC's wanted to rebel against the system they'd be libertarians or civic nationalists and they'd be fighting the excesses of corporate power even where it feeds the left wing ideologies of the world; they'd be combating multinationalism and globalism, not apparently backing them out of fear of Nazis. They'd be striving for the abolition of all censorship, not supporting its use so long as it aims to the "right."

I don't generally lose sleep though over the existence of these latte-drinking proletariat activists; they are small in number and short on physical efforts beyond hurling a rock or shouting at the police whenever they get together in groups larger than a dozen or so. Indeed, their prevalence in the now much-maligned social justice crusades of the new moral era have led to a far larger backlash wherein all the ideologies they most dislike are massively growing; this includes ethnic nationalism, civic nationalism, libertarianism, anarcho-capitalism, constitutionalism, classical liberalism, and even fringe elements of monarchism and literal fascism.

XI: Conclusion

Here thus I have offered my general opinion of communism- I cannot agree with the ideology, even if I believe that some communists have benevolence in their heads and hearts when they suggest making use of a communal system or something approximating or approaching it. The system itself is so diametrically opposed to evolutionary reality and has failed in so many ways when attempted that it is hardly worth bothering to use.

There are systems over time which have functioned to a degree of stability- some more than others- communism has so little that it is, even according to many communists, a case more of improper implementation than of its purest form lacking the qualities needed to operate and continue and grow. The presence of central planning destroys some regimes, and lack of organization destroys the rest- tens of millions have died and many more suffered under communist movements and parties, which show a marked and stunning brutality and authoritarian bent regardless of how "pure" they were or were not.

To write a book on the evils of communism would perhaps be difficult because those evils are so profuse and so often large in their scope. From the abject misery of peasants in Pol Pot's Cambodia to the death of thousands of civilians who were unfortunate enough to be born to upper class status during the early days of Stalin's reign, it seems the ideology is simply not capable of bringing good to the world and instead leaves only darkness and suffering in its wake only to eventually be thrown off by the same people that once rose up to implement it.